North to Oak Island

Dudley Bromley

A Pacemaker® Book

GLOE
Pearsoi

North to Oak Island

Dudley Bromley
AR B.L.: 3.4
Points: 1.0

UG

The PACEMAKER BESTSELLERS

Bestsellers I

Bestsellers II

Bestsellers III

Bestsellers IV

Series Director: Tom Belina
Designer: Richard Kharibian
Cover and illustrations: David Grove

ISBN 0-8224-5271-5

Printed in the United States of America

7 8 9 10 11   07 06 05 04 03   **1-800-321-3106**
                                        www.pearsonlearning.com

CONTENTS

CHAPTER 1

BRISTOL

It was dark.

Will Andrews finally reached the port city of Bristol, England. He was glad. He would not have to spend another night sleeping beside the road.

Will had left London two weeks ago, on April 9, 1732. He had walked all the way. It was more than a hundred miles. Will had taken his time. It was, after all, his last chance to see England.

Will was going to the New World, to America. That was why he had come to Bristol. Bristol was a very busy port city. Many ships came and went every day. Will planned to be on one of them.

Will had worked in a print shop in London since he was 13. For more than seven years he worked there. In that time, he learned all about printing and printing presses.

He had helped to print many books about the New World. And he had read them all many times. He had dreamed about the brave men who sailed across the Atlantic Ocean. He knew that one day he, too, would join them. And now that day was almost here.

Will walked toward the water where the tall ships were tied. About a block from the sea, he saw a small building. A sign on the building said "Shipping Office." It was the building that Will was looking for. He went up to the door. It was locked. The office was closed.

Then Will saw a list nailed to the wall outside the office. On it were the names of all the ships that would leave Bristol the next day. The list also told what time the ships would leave. And it said where they were going.

The names of nine ships were written on the list. Three of the ships were going north. Four were headed south. Only two were going west, to the New World.

One of the ships sailing west was called *Falcon II*. It was to leave at noon tomorrow. It was going to the Bahamas. But the list said *Falcon II* would take no one other than its own crew. There were no tickets for sale.

The other ship going west was called *Yorktown*. It was set to sail first thing in the morning. *Yorktown* was going to New York, and just a few tickets were left.

Will's ticket would cost him almost all of his money. But the ship was going to the New World, so it didn't matter. Besides, there was a note on the bottom of the list. It said *Falcon II* and *Yorktown* were the only ships going west for two weeks.

Will reached into his shirt to see if his money was still there. It was. He smiled at himself. He had made the same check every hour since he left London. He couldn't be too careful. It was all the money he had. He had saved many years for this day.

Will left the shipping office and walked toward the water. He planned to find *Yorktown*. When he did, he was going to buy his ticket right away.

Lots of people were all over the place. Will could hear singing on one side of the street. It sounded to him like a fight was going on on the other side.

Suddenly, a small man ran up and started walking along side of Will. He touched Will on the arm. "Keep walking," he said.

Will kept walking. "Who are you?" he asked.

The man didn't look at Will. "Never mind that. You want to buy a gold pocket watch?"

"No, thanks."

"How about a gun? You got a gun?"

"Well, no—"

"You should get one. Bristol is no place to be walking around without a gun, believe me."

The small man looked at Will for the first time. He smiled. Several of his teeth were missing.

Will started to laugh at the man. But before he could even begin, Will was pushed in between two buildings. The small man was very strong. And very fast. He had moved too fast for Will to get out of his way.

Then two other hands grabbed him by the arms. The little man had a friend helping him. Will tried to break free. But it was too late. The little man had a club in his hands. Will started to shout for help.

Then everything went black.

CHAPTER **2**

THE *FALCON II*

Will tasted blood.

His bottom lip was big and red. It hurt when he touched it. And there was a hard bump on his head. It hurt, too. In fact, Will hurt all over. He was cold and stiff from lying on the ground all night. All night!

Will jumped to his feet. However, everything suddenly started spinning around. He had to rest. His head felt like it was about to blow up.

Slowly he was able to move. He looked around. It was morning. The sun was high in the sky.

And *Yorktown* was gone. It had already sailed hours before.

Will shook his head. He felt sick. He had missed the ship. And another one would not leave for two weeks.

Then Will remembered about the small man with the funny teeth. He reached into his shirt. His money was gone, too. And so was the bag with all his clothes.

Now Will thought he would never get to the New World. He didn't know what he would do without any money. For a while, he thought about robbing someone himself. But he decided against it. If he should get caught, he would never get to the New World.

Then he walked past *Falcon II*. The ship's crew was busy carrying food, water, and other things on board.

Will remembered the list he had seen on the wall at the shipping office. It had said that *Falcon II* would not take anyone but its own crew. That gave Will an idea.

A big, tall man with a loud voice was shouting orders to the crew. They called him Max. Max had thick arms and legs and a chest like a drum. He wore a gun and held a cat-o'-nine-tails, which was a rope used to beat men.

Will walked up to Max, who turned and looked down at him. He was over six feet tall. When Max spoke, it seemed like he was shouting. "What do you want?"

"I want to join the crew, sir. Are you the Captain?"

Max looked at Will for a long time. Then he broke out laughing. He called other members of the crew over. He told them what Will had said, and they laughed, too.

Finally, Max stopped laughing. He wiped a tear from his eye. "No, I'm not the Captain. I'm just the First Mate. And I don't think you would like it on *Falcon II*."

"But I want to go to the New World, and—"

"Sorry. We have all the crew we need. And then some. You will have to find another ship, my boy."

Will wanted to say something else. But the First Mate turned to face his crew.

"All right, back to work. If we push off late, the Captain will use our hides for a sail."

There were still many things to be put on the ship. Will hung around for a while, watching. But he couldn't just stand there all day long.

He had to do something. He was going to get to the New World, no matter what.

Then he had another idea. He would hide on board and wait until the ship was far out to sea. Then he would show himself and ask to join the crew. They would have to let him stay. What else could they do?

Will didn't want to think about the answer to that one. Besides, he had already made up his mind. It was the only thing he could do. He would have to become a stowaway.

When Max turned his back and the others were working on board, Will climbed into a big box. The box was sitting with many others that were about to be put on board. The box was packed with rags and old sails. It would make a nice home for a few days.

Soon he could feel the box being lifted. And when the box stopped, Will could hear men walking away. He lifted the top and looked out. The box was in *Falcon II's* hold. Will had made it on board the ship. He closed the box and sat back to rest. In a few minutes, he was sleeping.

The next thing Will knew, he could feel the ship going up and down and hear waves splash-

ing. He knew he was out to sea at last. He was on his way to the New World.

For the next week, Will stayed down in the hold. There he found several big bottles of water and of rum. He also found dry meat and hard bread. And many guns. And cannonballs. And lots of black gunpowder.

And rats.

Will woke up one morning, and a big brown rat was looking him right in the eye. That was when he decided he was tired of staying below deck.

CHAPTER 3

STOWAWAY

Will slowly opened the trap door to the ship's hold. He was surprised by the number of men he could see. The First Mate, Max, had been right. *Falcon II* had all of the men it needed.

Suddenly, the trap door was lifted all the way open. Two big men were standing over Will. One of the men was pointing a gun at him. "Well, what have we here?" said the man with the gun.

The other man turned around and shouted to the First Mate. "Max!" he called. "Look here—a stowaway!"

Everyone on the deck stopped what they were doing and made a circle around Will.

The First Mate walked over to Will. He shook his head. He reached down and grabbed Will by the coat. His eyes were full of fire. He pulled Will up with one hand. Will thought it best not to try to fight back.

"Throw him over the side!" someone shouted. "Show him what we do with stowaways! Over the side with him!"

Max pushed Will to the side of the ship. Before Will knew what was happening, he was hanging over the side, head down. Max was holding him by the legs. Everyone was laughing and shouting and having a good time. Everyone but Will, that is. He thought he was finished for sure. He had made a big mistake stowing away on the *Falcon II*. That was for sure.

But then Max pulled Will up and let him fall on the deck. "Go and get the Captain," he told a member of the crew.

Will was on his back. Max was watching his eyes. Will knew that he had better not make any more mistakes. The next thing he did or said had to be the *right* thing. But what *was* the right thing? He didn't know. And he just couldn't seem to think straight. So he didn't do anything. He just lay there, waiting.

Then he saw the ship's flag. It wasn't the same flag that had hung from the mast in Bristol. In Bristol, the flag had been a Union Jack, the British flag. Now, however, there was a black flag flying over the ship.

Will knew that the black flag was called a Jolly Roger. He also knew that a Jolly Roger was used only by pirates. Will was a stowaway on a pirate ship!

"What is going on here?" came a loud call.

Will started to turn and see who was talking. But he was suddenly lifted to his feet. Max had grabbed him again.

"Stand up and face the Captain, stowaway!" Max said.

The Captain came forward and stood in front of Will. Will looked at the Captain and couldn't believe his eyes.

The Captain was a *woman.*

She was not as tall as Will, but she was twice as wide. She wore several guns and held a big cutlass in her right hand. Her clothes were all black, and she had wild black hair. She had a gold ring in one ear and an ugly red mark on her neck. Her teeth were yellow, and she looked mean as a wild animal.

"I've often wondered what I would do if I ever found a stowaway," she said. Her voice sounded like two rocks being rubbed together. "Now is a good time to find out."

Will was trying to think. He had read about a woman pirate in a book he helped to print last year. What had the book called her? Will couldn't remember.

Then it came to him. He stood up straight. "I'm not a stowaway, Captain Kate, ma'am."

Everyone seemed surprised that Will knew who he was talking to. The Captain herself seemed most surprised. "You know who I am?" she asked Will.

"Yes, ma'am. You're Captain Kate. Also called Black Kate. The Spanish almost hanged you last year. Only you got away. But I thought your ship was called *Revenge.*"

"It is. *Falcon II* is just a name I use in some ports. However, the question here is not the name of my ship."

"Make him walk the plank!" came a call from the crew.

Will knew that he had just one chance. He had to win the Captain to his side. And it looked like he would have to lie in order to do it. "Captain Kate, ma'am," he said. "I think you are the best pirate who ever lived. I've spent years dreaming about the day I could join your crew. I want to be a pirate, too."

Many of the men started to laugh. But Kate made them stop with just a look. Then she turned back to Will. "You can see I'm not short of men. And you don't look like a pirate to me. Do you take me for a fool?"

Will's plan didn't seem to be working. So he decided to try something different. He decided to stop telling lies. "Please, Captain. Give me a chance. I just want to get to the New World, that's all. Let me work my way there as a crew member. I'm good with my hands. I can read and write, too. And I've a good head for numbers. There must be something I can do."

Captain Kate walked in a big circle around the deck of the ship. She looked at Will, then at her crew, then back at Will again. She took out a pipe and started to smoke. She played with the ring in her ear. No one said anything.

The only sound was the sound of the wind in the sails on the masts above. That and the sound of the waves splashing against the sides of the ship.

Will could feel his heart pounding in his chest. It was pounding so hard he could almost hear it. He tried to tell what the Captain was thinking. But her face was like stone. He waited for her to say something. So did the crew.

Finally, she put away the pipe. She came over to Will. "Well, my boy," she said. "I've made up my mind."

CHAPTER 4

LOG OF THE *REVENGE*

"From now on you keep the ship's log," the Captain said.

Will could tell that Max did not like what Captain Kate had decided. When the Captain gave her order, Max just shook his head. Then he walked away. Most of the other members of the crew did the same thing. They would all much rather have seen Will walk the plank.

"I don't write in the log every day like I should," said the Captain. She and Will were alone now. They were on their way to her cabin below deck. "And you're the only other one on board who can read or write."

"I'll write a page every day," said Will. "Maybe more."

"You'll write just what I tell you and nothing else," Captain Kate said.

"Yes, ma'am."

At the door to her cabin, Captain Kate stopped. "By the way," she said. "Pirates and people who have always wanted to be pirates don't say 'Yes, ma'am.' They say 'Aye, Captain.' Got that?"

Will could feel himself turning red. "Yes, ma—" he said, stopping himself. "I mean, aye, Captain."

Kate laughed and went into her cabin. Will followed her in and closed the door. The Captain went to her desk. She picked up a bottle and took a drink from it. She drank again. Then she turned to Will, wiping her mouth with her hand. "What might your name be?"

"Will. Will Andrews."

"Would you like some rum, Will Andrews?"

"No, thank you," he said. "I don't drink."

Kate shook her head. "You have a lot to learn about being a pirate," she said. Then she laughed and took another long drink from the bottle. When the bottle was empty, she took out a key. She opened a big strong box next to her desk. "The log is kept in this box," she said.

She pulled out a large black book and handed it to Will. The book was the ship's log. Kate had already written in half of the book. Her notes covered the past three years. Will looked forward to reading all of it later.

"For today," said Captain Kate, "write about yourself. Tell how you were found out and then joined the crew. Say that you were put in charge of the log. Then add that you had better stay out of trouble and do what you are told. Write that if you don't, you will walk the plank. And keep what's in the log to yourself. Got all of that?"

"Aye, Captain." Will sat down and started to write in the log.

For the next six weeks, while *Revenge* sailed across the Atlantic, Will kept the ship's log. In that time, he learned a lot about *Revenge's* Captain, Black Kate.

In the ship's log, Will read how *Revenge* had sailed all over the New World. It had sailed from Nova Scotia in the north to Colombia in South America. Of most interest to Will were the ports in North America. *Revenge* had stopped at Charleston, Boston, Philadelphia, and New York. And that was just last year.

The list of ships that *Revenge* had robbed was long, too. When Will added up what Kate and her crew had taken last summer alone, it came to millions.

The Captain had written again and again about her "secret island." She never said where it was. But she made it sound like it was in some part of the New World.

Much of what Will learned about Kate came from her crew. They had little to do on the long trip. During the day, a lot of time was spent shooting fish, most often sharks. Nights were spent below deck, playing cards and drinking rum and telling stories. That was when the men most liked to talk about their Captain.

Kate was not her real name. No one knew what her real name was. No one knew how old she was, either. Some men thought she came from Bristol, but no one was sure. But everyone knew for a fact that she had been a very good friend of Captain Kidd, the famous pirate. Many of them could remember her crying the day Captain Kidd was hanged.

Some said that Kate had won *Revenge* in a card game. Others said that she made off with it from a Spanish port one dark night. Still others said that she had had the ship made in the Bahamas from her own plans.

Will wondered why someone didn't just *ask* the Captain where she got her ship. The crew members laughed. "You don't ask Captain Kate *nothing* that isn't any of your business," one man told him. "The Captain don't like people asking her questions."

As for Kate's secret island, the crew thought it was real. Each time *Revenge's* holds were filled with treasure, Kate stopped robbing. She put most of her crew off at New Providence in the Bahamas. Then she left. Only Max and a few others went with her. The ship was gone for ten weeks and always came back empty. She was putting her treasure somewhere. The crew was sure of that. But they had no idea where.

It seemed that Will learned something new every day. And many things happened on the Atlantic crossing that he would never forget. But there was one day that Will would remember above all others. That day was June 3, 1732. It was a very special day for everyone on board *Revenge.*

To Captain Kate, it was just another day in the life of a pirate. But to the crew it was a day of sharks and guns and gold. And to Will, it was the day of the cat-o'-nine-tails.

It was also the day *Revenge* reached the New World.

CHAPTER **5**

A TASTE OF THE CAT

At noon on June 3, Will got his first look at the New World. He was on watch, high up on the ship's mast. He was looking into a spyglass. He could see a dot in the distance. It looked like it was floating on the water. Then he saw another dot. Then another. The dots were islands. *Revenge* had reached the Bahamas.

"Land ho!" Will shouted as loud as he could.

The crew came running up on deck. Everyone was trying to see the land. There was a lot of laughing and singing.

Then something frightening happened.

One of the members of the crew, a man called Jacob, fell over the side. Several others worked to fish Jacob out of the water with ropes. Jacob could swim well and was finally able to reach one of the ropes. He grabbed for it. By then, however, it was too late.

From his place high above everything, Will was the first one to see the trouble. He pointed to the water, not far from Jacob. He shouted as loud as he could. "Sharks!" he shouted. "Sharks!"

Many shots rang out. The crew was able to shoot several sharks. But for every one they shot, two more showed up.

Then Jacob screamed, and the water around him turned red. When he was finally pulled on board, both his legs and one arm were gone. He wanted to die. He begged to be killed, and Captain Kate shot him.

Will climbed down off the mast as fast as he could. He did not feel very well. He wanted to lie down and rest. But he knew it would be better to keep busy. He decided to write down what had happened in the ship's log.

The Captain was not back in her cabin yet. But the door was open. Will went in and got the log out of the box by her desk.

He saw an open chest sitting on the desk. There were many gold coins in the chest and lots of jewels. There were also two pieces of paper, both yellow with age. One of the papers was a map. The other was a drawing of some kind, perhaps a set of plans. Will could not read the words on either paper.

Suddenly, Kate was standing in the door. "Will!" she said in an angry voice. "What do you think you're doing?"

"I'm sorry, Captain," said Will, dropping the papers. "I came in here to write in the log . . ."

"You should never have looked at those papers."

"I'm sorry, Captain. Really, I am. But it doesn't even matter. I couldn't read any of it. It wasn't written in English. Besides, I wouldn't tell anyone even if I could read it. I gave you my word on it."

"Still, you put your nose where it doesn't belong. For that you must taste the cat-o'-nine-tails. Word or no word."

"But, Cap—"

"I'm sure Max would be glad to give you a hundred blows. But ten will do for now. And if you ever tell anyone what you saw in that chest . . ."

"I won't, Captain. I promise. I won't."

Kate came close to him. She pulled out a gun and pointed it at Will's face. "If you do," she said, "I'll shoot you like I shot Jacob. Only you will be begging me *not* to shoot. Now, get up on deck. Your beating begins in five minutes."

Up on the deck, Max tied Will to a post in the hot sun. Then he tore the shirt from Will's back and threw it on the deck.

Will jumped when the cat-o'-nine-tails hit him. It had hurt much more than he thought it would. It had hurt more than anything else he had ever felt before. And it was beginning to burn like fire. Will's eyes filled with tears and he wanted to scream.

The second blow hurt even more than the first. The third time he was hit, it was all he could do to keep from screaming. He didn't think he could take the rest of the blows. He thought he would go mad.

Then Will was saved. From far away came the sound of cannons. The man on watch shouted down to the Captain. "Ships! One flying Spanish colors, the other a Jolly Roger!"

Kate stopped Max. She sent her crew to their stations. She freed the ropes that held Will to the post. "I'm cutting seven off your sentence," she said. "Find a gun now, and don't be slow about it."

Then Kate pulled a spyglass from her pocket and looked across the water. "That is Niles Kinneman's ship or I'm not Black Kate," she said. "I'll bet he is surprised to see *us!*"

Max handed Will a shirt and a gun. The First Mate looked at Will a different way now. So did the rest of the crew. It looked like they had decided to welcome him into their private group. He found out why later. They had all tasted the cat-o'nine-tails at one time or another. Even Max.

Captain Kate laughed. She was still looking into the spyglass. "Niles Kinneman is a good pirate. He has just robbed a Spanish treasure ship. He took a lot of gold from the Spanish. Now we shall take it all from him."

CHAPTER **6**

RED SKY AT MORNING

"Niles Kinneman's ship is called *Neptune,*" said Kate. "It's not as big as *Revenge.* It's not as fast, either."

The Captain was right. *Revenge* closed in fast on *Neptune.* Both ships fired their cannons. But *Revenge* had much more power. Cannonballs from *Revenge's* guns tore holes in *Neptune's* sails. Finally, Captain Kate's guns knocked the other ship's mast down.

Revenge pulled up next to *Neptune.* Men were jumping from ship to ship, fighting with guns and cutlasses. Niles Kinneman's crew put up a good fight. But there were too many on Kate's side. For each man that Kate lost, Niles Kinneman lost ten or more.

Sharks began to swim between the ships. They were waiting for men to fall in the water. And many men did fall. Some fell when they got hurt. Others tripped or were pushed. Either way, the sharks got them.

Will stayed out of the fight for a long time. But then two men jumped him from behind. The Captain shot one of them and came at the other one with her cutlass. The second man ran away and jumped back toward the *Neptune's* deck. His jump was too short, however, and he fell toward the sharks with a scream.

"Thanks, Captain!" Will shouted above the noise of the fighting.

Soon, just a few members of *Neptune's* crew were left. Niles Kinneman was one of them, but even he was hurt. He had been shot in the leg. He and his men gave up.

Kate ordered her men to take the gold and jewels from *Neptune's* holds. Then she ordered Niles Kinneman and his men into a longboat. She gave them enough water for a week, then let them go.

Niles Kinneman shouted at Kate until he was too far away to be heard. "I'll get even with you for this!" he screamed. "I'll track you

down, Black Kate. I'll find you, and I'll get even. You wait and see. I'll get you!"

Kate just laughed at Niles Kinneman. Then she set his ship on fire and ordered *Revenge* to sail away. *Neptune* was seen burning well into the night.

Will could still see the smoke from the fire when he went on watch the next morning. The sun had just come up. The sky was red. A red sky in the morning was supposed to mean bad weather.

Late that afternoon, it started to rain. The wind began to blow. Waves pounded against the ship.

The storm got worse and worse. The sky grew dark. It looked like night. *Revenge* rocked up and down in the water like a toy. The wind was blowing so hard that the sails had to be taken down so they wouldn't tear off.

Revenge was caught in the worst kind of storm, a hurricane. The hurricane lasted the rest of that day and all of that night. No one on board *Revenge* got any sleep. The ship was rolling too much for that. So the crew sat around drinking rum and telling stories below deck. Even the Captain joined in.

Will enjoyed the crew's talk. But by far the best talk came from Captain Kate herself. She had a surprise for her crew. A big one.

Outside, the hurricane was at its worst. But inside, no one paid it any mind. This was not the first time they had to ride out a hurricane. All eyes were on the Captain.

"As you all know," she began, "I've been a pirate for many years. I've robbed too many ships to name. I've taken more gold than any of you has ever seen at once."

She stopped long enough to light her pipe and take a drink. Then she went on. "At first I liked being a pirate. Not only did it make me rich, but I had a lot of fun besides. Now, however, I'm tired of it. I don't want to be a pirate any more. I didn't want to say anything before. I didn't want you to get any wrong ideas. But this is our last trip together. I'm leaving the sea."

Once again, Kate stopped talking. She smoked her pipe and looked around at her men. No one said anything.

"There is still the matter of my treasure," Kate said at last. "At present, it sits out of sight in a cave. But what is to become of it? I have more treasure than all of us could ever spend."

Several men shook their heads like they couldn't believe what they heard. "However," said the Captain, "I also have a set of plans. I got them from Captain Kidd himself. He told me that Leonardo da Vinci drew the plans. Leonardo da Vinci was an Italian who lived two hundred years ago. His plans show how to bury a treasure so it can never be reached by anyone else. These plans have been used on my secret island. Everything there is ready. I could bury my treasure in just a few minutes. Then no one would ever be able to get to it without the plans. No matter *how* hard they tried."

Will thought back to the day before. He had seen the plans in Kate's cabin. They were with the map in the chest on her desk. He had tasted the cat-o'-nine-tails because of them.

The Captain went on. "I was going to bury all of the treasure. But things have changed." The Captain looked at Max and smiled. Max smiled back. "In the end," said Kate, "I'll still bury most of it. But not *all* of it. You can thank Max for that. He was good enough to make me remember my crew."

On that last word, every man in the ship sat up, their eyes wide.

"You men have worked hard for me," Captain Kate went on. "You have all been paid well, it's true. But you should get more. Because you are the best. And you will, too. I promise that you will all be rich."

Everyone broke into wide smiles as the Captain ended her talk. There was a lot of happy whispering going on. A few men shouted with joy. The crew drank to Kate and threw themselves a party. No one thought about the storm outside.

It was not a night for worry.

CHAPTER **7**

NEW PROVIDENCE

The hurricane was gone by the next morning. The sky was clear and blue. The sun was bright and warm. The sea sent slow waves rolling toward *Revenge*. The ship had come out of the hurricane with only a few ropes torn away. The men on watch were already fixing them.

Will woke up outside Captain Kate's cabin. He had the ship's log in his hand. He must have gone to sleep trying to write everything down. He opened the book and laughed. He had passed out before he finished even one word.

Will stood up. He felt better than he thought he would. As a matter of fact, he was hungry, *very* hungry.

After breakfast, the Captain asked everyone to meet on the deck. Some crew members thought she was going to take back everything she said last night. Max, however, was quick to put an end to that talk.

When everyone was ready, Captain Kate stepped before them. "Men," she said. "Everything I said last night still holds true. But before we set sail for the treasure, we must stop in New Providence. I, for one, am sick of the food on this ship. I want to get us some chickens and some cows. I want lots of fresh fruits and vegetables. And I want a real cook. This is a special trip we are about to begin. It will be my last trip as a pirate, and I plan to enjoy it."

The Captain ordered a course set for New Providence Island. The hurricane had sent *Revenge* far out to sea. It took a full three weeks to reach the island. Then the ship sailed into the only port city on the island. The city was also called New Providence.

"It doesn't look like much of a city," said Will. He was standing on the deck with Captain Kate and Max. The Captain was about to go into town. Will was looking for a chance to ask if he could go with her.

"Aye, that's true," said Kate. "There are no real stores or homes or schools here. Not much of anything. Only taverns."

"What kind of taverns?"

"Places where pirates like to hang out. The only law in New Providence is pirate law. It's every man for himself in this town."

"I hope someone is going with you."

Kate smiled at Will. "Aye. Max and ten of my best men." She looked at Will with one eye closed. "Well, what is it, Will? You're wanting to say something, I can tell."

Will looked out at the buildings of the city. "Aye, Captain," he said. "I'd like to go with you. More than anything, Captain. To you it's just New Providence. But to me, it's more—it's the New World."

Captain Kate thought for a minute. Then she said, "All right. You can come along. But stay close. And stay out of trouble."

Will broke into a big smile. "Aye, Captain!"

The landing party left *Revenge* and walked into New Providence. Kate sent two of the men to buy some fresh food and hire a cook. Then the Captain took Will and the others to her favorite tavern.

The tavern was filled with people. The room was big. It smelled like rum, smoke, and old shoes. The crowd was loud. There were card games and drinks and painted women all over the place. Several kinds of music were being played at once.

Kate moved across the room. Her men followed. Many people in the crowd seemed to know the Captain. But very few of them said anything to her.

She found an empty table and sat down. Max and Will and two others sat with her. The rest of the landing party stood around the table. Kate ordered a jug of rum for each man.

When the drinks came, Kate put some of her rum in a cup. Then she pulled out a small bag of gunpowder. She put some of the gunpowder in the cup. It floated on top of the rum.

Next, Captain Kate stood up and shouted for everyone to stop talking. Slowly, the noise in the tavern stopped.

"Here is something my friend, the late Captain Kidd, showed me," she called out. Now all eyes were on her.

Then Kate set fire to her drink. The gunpowder went off like a small cannon. The

Captain held her cup high so everyone could see the fire and smoke. Then she laughed and drank it all down at once.

Will was pleased with the Captain's trick. He was about to call out for her to do it again. Then a gun went off.

Everyone in the tavern turned toward the door in surprise.

Niles Kinneman was standing there with several of his men. Before, he had been shot in the leg. Now that leg was missing. He wore a piece of wood there instead.

Kinneman held two guns, one in each hand. One of the guns was still smoking from being fired. The other was ready to shoot.

"So, Black Kate," he said. "We meet again!"

CHAPTER **8**

THE COOK

All of a sudden, Kate grabbed a jug of rum. She threw it at Niles Kinneman. The jug hit him in the arm, and his other gun went off. It was a wild shot in the air.

The next thing Will knew, everyone in the tavern was fighting. Men and chairs and tables were all flying across the room. Everyone and everything was crashing into everything and everyone. Men were shouting and women were screaming. Everywhere things were breaking and being smashed. The noise in the tavern was like a slow explosion.

Before Will could even think of joining in, he was hit from behind. He fell down. When he started to get up, a fat man jumped off a table on top of him. He was knocked out.

When Will came to, Max was carrying him. "Some pirate you are," Max said to him. Max was running toward the ship. Captain Kate was at his side. She was laughing like a mad woman. She thought the fight had been great fun.

Most of the rest of the landing party was right behind them. Two men, however, never did make it back to the ship.

Revenge was ready to sail as soon as the landing party got there. Max put Will down and helped the crew to push off. Will knew that night was not a safe time for any ship to leave port. But right now it was the best thing for them to do.

It was also the only thing for them to do.

Kate was studying the sky. It was very dark. "Luck is with us," she said. "There is a good wind and no moon tonight."

Then Will spoke for the first time in a while. "What happened?" he said. "Why wasn't anyone on our side?"

"Those men can't stand the thought of a woman pirate," said Captain Kate. "They all hate me. I'm better than they are, and they know it. They were glad when Niles Kinneman showed up. They were just looking for a reason to fight."

"Aye," said Max. "They hate the Captain, all right. But they would love to get at her treasure. They would sell their own mothers for one look at Kate's map."

At last, Kate took out her pipe and began to smoke. "We have made a clean escape," she said. "By the time the sun comes up, we will be long gone. It will be too late for anyone to try and follow us."

The next morning, *Revenge's* new cook fixed breakfast for everyone. It was the best food any of them had ever tasted.

The ship took five weeks to go north from the Bahamas to Nova Scotia. Summer was almost gone. The crew, of course, was ready for the trip to be over. They were looking forward to seeing the Captain's treasure.

Just before dark, on September 12, 1732, Kate called the crew together. As always, they met on the ship's deck.

Revenge was in sight of a small island. The Captain pointed it out to her crew. It was still very far away. "It's called Oak Island," she told them. "We will be there in the morning."

Will heard a noise behind him while Kate was talking. It sounded like a fight was going on. He turned to see what was happening.

Max was pushing the ship's new cook toward the front of the ship. The First Mate tripped the cook and then kicked him.

"Get up!" Max shouted. "The Captain will decide what is to be done with you."

Not one of the crew members could understand why Max was so angry. Even the Captain seemed surprised. "What's the trouble, Max?" she asked.

"I caught this dog throwing trash over the side, Captain. He was letting it float away, like it was nothing!"

Will didn't think that was anything to get so angry about. But the Captain went wild. She turned red and screamed at the cook. "You dog!" she shouted. "You know that you are supposed to sink our trash."

"I'm sorry, Captain," said the cook. "I forgot. I just forgot."

"You forgot!" said Kate. She pulled out her cutlass. She pushed the point up against the cook's neck. "You have been letting it float away all along, haven't you?"

The cook was very afraid. He didn't say anything. Kate took a step toward him. Her cutlass made a small cut on the man's neck. Blood ran down the front of his shirt.

"Who put you up to this?" Kate wanted to know. "Was it Niles Kinneman? Is that who you left the floating trail for?"

"No one put me up to it," said the cook. "I just forgot, that's all. I just forgot."

"Too bad," said the Captain. "Because now you must walk the plank. Take him away, Max."

"Aye, Captain," said Max. He pulled the cook to one side. He tied the man's legs together and his hands behind his back with a piece of rope. The cook began to cry.

A board was moved into place. It was sticking out over the water. Max picked the cook up and dropped him on the board. He pushed the man out over the water.

"Please, Captain," the cook said. "I can't swim all tied up like this."

"It wouldn't matter, even if you could swim. No one has ever escaped the sharks in these waters."

Then Kate picked up a long pole. She used it to push the cook toward the end of the plank.

The man fell into the water with a splash and sank from sight.

When that was over, Kate turned to her crew. "We have no time to waste," she said. "Niles Kinneman and the others will show up soon. Mark my words. They have all been looking for a chance to get at my treasure. And now the cook has given it to them. We must get to Oak Island right away."

CHAPTER **9**

OAK ISLAND

Oak Island was like a beautiful dream in the morning light.

It was high and wide and green. It was a big rolling hill made of sand and rocks. The whole island was covered with grass and trees and other green plants. Drops of water were on all of the plants, and the morning sun made them shine like little stars.

The sea around Oak Island was not very deep. *Revenge* had come as close as it could get. The crew would have to go the last several hundred yards in longboats.

Will rode in the last boat with Max. There were not as many men in their boat as in the others. Their boat was filled with tools and guns and rum. They also had lots of gunpowder.

Will held onto the ship's log with both hands. The Captain had ordered him to bring it, but she had not said why. And Will had learned long ago not to question her.

Kate's boat was the first to land on the island. She had a fire built while she and her men waited for the others. One by one, the other boats landed.

Then Captain Kate took a burning stick from the fire. With the secret plans and map in her other hand, she led the way. She took her men toward a small mountain of rocks by the water not far away.

The Captain walked in a circle around the big pile of rocks. Every few feet she would stop and look at her secret papers. Then she found an opening. "Here it is," she said.

Kate gave Will the burning stick to hold. Then she turned to her crew. "This opening leads to a tunnel, which leads to the treasure. The tunnel was built by Captain Kidd's men. They did all the work on Oak Island. Captain Kidd had planned to hide his own treasure here. But he never got the chance. His crew, of course, took his treasure for themselves after he was hanged."

Kate put Max in charge of the crew, and he put the men to work. Kate then took Will and six others into the tunnel with her. The men carried kegs of gunpowder. Kate also carried two kegs of gunpowder.

Will led the way in the dark tunnel. He was carrying the only light they had. "When we are finished with the treasure," said Kate, "this tunnel will be closed. Closed for good. Falling rocks will shut it off from the outside. And water will fill it from the inside. Then the tunnel can never be used again."

Before long, the tunnel opened up into a large cave. Kate put the two kegs of gunpowder down by the opening. She took the light from Will and held it high. Everyone in the cave made soft sounds of surprise and wonder.

The yellow shine of gold was all over the place. And there were millions of jewels, all colors, like stars on a clear night. There were chests filled with treasure, piled three high in some places. Chest after chest, row upon row. Even the floor of the cave was covered with gold and jewels.

Kate took the burning stick. She used it to light an oil lamp on the wall of the cave. She

pointed to three great chests, all filled with jewels. She told the men who came with her and Will to take the chests outside. She gave one of them a lamp, and they followed her orders.

Then Kate turned to Will. "Give me the log," she said, holding out her hand.

Will handed her the book. She took it and looked around until she found a small chest. "This is a special chest. It will keep the log dry when the cave is filled with water. The secret of Oak Island will stay dry and safe."

"You never plan to come back here, do you?"

Kate let out a long laugh. "Of course not," she said. "I'm rich besides what I have here. I'm doing this for the *fun* of it. Think about what it will be like hundreds of years from now. Men will still be trying to get at my treasure."

Kate put her secret plans and map into the chest with the log. Then she closed the small chest and put it down. "Let's go," she said.

She stopped at the opening to the tunnel. Will helped her to push a big rock in front of the opening. Then she opened both kegs of gunpowder. One keg she turned over and left there. The other she used to leave a trail of gunpowder behind her.

Back in the light of day, Will saw the crew standing around the three chests. It sounded like they were throwing a party. One by one, they would go up to a chest. Then they would grab as many jewels as they could carry.

"Go ahead," Kate said to Will. "Take as much as you want, too. There's enough for everyone."

Will didn't need to be told twice.

Suddenly, however, the crew's fun was ended. From far away came the roar of cannons.

Kate took out a spyglass and climbed a big rock. Many shots rang out. Then there was nothing. When Kate climbed down, she didn't say anything to her crew. She walked over to Max. She was very angry. *"Revenge* is sinking," she said. "And Niles Kinneman did it!"

CHAPTER 10

ALL IS WELL

Kate touched the burning stick to the gun-powder. The powder caught fire and burned its way toward the tunnel.

Then several explosions shook the island. The mountain of rocks fell down. The sea, which had been held back, rushed in suddenly with a low roar. Water covered everything on that part of the island.

The Captain ordered her crew back to their boats. "Maine is just across the Bay of Fundy," she told them. "Three days at the most."

The crew, of course, took their jewels with them. They were all rich men now. Now they were the ones who had to look out for pirates.

Down by their boats, Will and the others could see three ships out to sea. The ships were all flying black flags. Kate's crew could also see many longboats on their way to Oak Island. *Revenge's* crew got off the island without any trouble. Will rode in the same boat with Max and the Captain.

Two of the boats were lost when a storm of cannonballs was fired at them, smashing them to bits. Then two more were hit. That left just Kate's boat and one other from *Revenge.*

Niles Kinneman's pirates, however, suddenly lost interest in Kate and her crew. All of their boats turned toward Oak Island at once. Will could see more than 20 of them. It was like a race had started.

And when the boats landed, pirates ran all over the island. Everyone was looking for some sign of where to dig for treasure.

Kate laughed at them until she turned red. "Poor dogs," she said at last. "Little do they know. My ship was not called *Revenge* for nothing. My revenge is that no one will ever get to my treasure. No one!"

Kate laughed and laughed. She was still laughing when the sun went down.

Early in the morning of the third day, Max stood up in the boat and pointed. "Land ho!" he said. "Maine, at last!"

Everyone looked to the west and smiled. They had crossed the Bay of Fundy and would soon land in Maine. True, they were all very hungry. But they were safe. And they still had their jewels.

Suddenly they heard the sound of cannons. First one, then many. Kate took out her spyglass and looked into it.

"It's them!" she said. "It's Niles Kinneman and his friends." She closed the spyglass and waved it in the air. "They found out they can't get at my treasure. So now *they* want revenge."

Will watched as a cannonball hit the other boat. The boat broke into many pieces. The men who could swim headed for land. Two others were pulled aboard Kate's boat. The rest went under.

Will turned to look at Kate. She was talking to Max in the back of the boat.

Suddenly, a cannonball flew out of nowhere. Will saw it out of the corner of his eye. He saw it smash Max in the chest. He heard a loud crack. Then Max was gone.

"Max!" screamed Kate. Another cannonball landed right behind her. It crashed into the

floor of the boat. Seconds later, everyone was in the water.

Will went for land. He kept his eye on the Captain, who could not swim as fast as he could.

When Kate got too far behind, Will went back for her. She seemed tired. "It's no use, Will," she said. "I never could swim very well."

Will grabbed her and pulled her behind him. "Don't worry, Captain," he said. "I'll save you. I will. Just hang on."

Soon they reached land. Will pulled the Captain out of the water. Then he saw that she was hurt.

"I think I fell on my cutlass when the boat was sinking," she said. She sounded very weak. It was a long time before she said anything else. "Thanks for trying."

Will felt his eyes filling with tears. "Everything is going to be all right, Captain," he said.

"Aye, Will," she said. "All is well."

Kate smiled once.

And then she was dead. Will sat there beside her, crying. He sat there until it started to get dark. Then he dug a hole to bury Kate in.

Then next morning, Will made his way south. As he walked, he thought about everything that had happened to him. It had not been an easy way to get to the New World. However, he got enough jewels out of it to start his own print shop. That was more than he had had when he started.

But best of all, Will Andrews was in the New World. And that was all he had ever wanted in the first place.

* * * *

This story is fiction, but the treasure of Oak Island is real. Someone went to a lot of trouble to bury something there. No one knows what it is or when it was put there. But people have been trying to dig it up for more than two hundred years.